RHYMES
for the MIND

Illuminate

your face

and your gaze

will make their days

Smile

RHYMES
for the MIND

SHARRON GREEN

Cover Photo: Sharron Green
Sunflower & Daisy drawing: Heather Moulson
Author Photo: Hattie Stewart-Darling @hattie_darling

You can find Sharron Green on social media:
Instagram, Facebook, Threads, X & TikTok @ Rhymes_n_Roses
Website: https://rhymesnroses.com

Independently published in 2025

Author's Note

Rhymes for the Mind is a collection of poems written to help ease the mind and process life today. It champions positivity and contemplation, enjoying the moment and the healing properties of time. Above all it is an invitation to love life and accept, and even embrace, change.

In sum, it is my approach to living, set to poetry.

It features various poetry forms including the elfchen; kyrielle; lokheeflip4; loop poem; pantoum; rondeau and a number of sonnets.

I'm pleased to say that a few of these pieces have already appeared elsewhere, and I am grateful to those involved in their selection. They are: 'Daylight Delight' in *The Dawntreader*; 'Harvest of Hope' in the Winter 2024 edition of *The Healer* from the Harry Edwards Foundation; 'Divine Midnight' in the *The Mum Poet Club – Guide to Self Care*.

In addition, 'The Roundabout Way' is also in my first pamphlet, *Introducing Rhymes_n_Roses* and 'A Stoic's View' is in *Viral Odes*, written during the pandemic.

Thank you for reading. I'd be very grateful for a review and to know your thoughts as a reader or writer of poetry. Plus, if you have enjoyed *Rhymes for the Mind* please take a look at my other publications.

@rhymes_n_roses

Contents

The Journey Out

Unlace the rope,
embrace the flow.

Gently ripple on silken tide,
beatific bobbing,
dreamy detachment.

Shush the turbulent voices,
in this no-man's zone,
in this anyone's haven.

Breathe
and breathe again.

No need to choose a port.
Let it choose you.

Where you gravitate
is your destiny.

Out of the Dark

Out of the dark, the blues of deep winter,
when we feel trapped and moods crash and splinter,

hope forces life to bud at twig's end,
glimpses of spring flirt just round the bend.

Bright yellow pops from ripe daffodils,
blossom unfurls and joyfully spills.

Out of the dark, we shrug off the night,
freed from within we greet the sunlight.

April Loops the Loop

Spring is born of hope
Hope that bounces bright
Bright like bold green shoots
Shoots that seek the light

Light shines spreading joy
Joy at nature's charm
Charm of fresh new life
Life pricks through the calm

Calm leaves branch and twig
Twig then bursts forth fronds
Fronds bud into spray
Spray dots polka ponds

Ponds brew bubble birth
Birth that makes you sing
Sing a song of hope
Hope is born in spring

My Dream Stream

I woke elated from a dream,
with pure emotion, eyes a-stream.
The setting was so very fair,
I couldn't wait to be back there.

I didn't know the way to there,
I had no map to be quite fair.
In truth it was a splendid stream,
but who knows where? It was a dream.

The next time that I had that dream,
I took a photo of the stream.
My photographic flair was fair,
but like all dreams I left it there.

I hatched a plan to get to there,
when I set off the day was fair.
Resolved to find a real stream,
a chocolate one, like in the dream.

Blank Canvas

Paint the sky to match your mood
    blue, grey, sunshine gold.

Colour in your deep desires
    look, leap and be bold.

Cast away your doubts and fears
    bury them in cloud.

If there's cause to celebrate
    make that rainbow loud.

When you need a moment's calm
    shroud yourself in white.

Shelter in the shade you've made
    watch as it gets light.

Magic Moments

Imagine rolling in the deep
Lonesome tonight you start to weep
The stairway up to heaven's steep
Like magic, music soothes your soul

The windmills of your mind whizz by
An unchained melody flies high
A candle in the wind may sigh
Like magic, music soothes your soul

Walking on sunshine burns your toes
Comf'tably numb all feeling goes
But sometimes when we touch truth flows
Like magic, music soothes your soul

The best of my love's what I bring
I have a dream, a song to sing
So, stand by me and be my king
Like magic, music soothes your soul

The Roundabout Way

'What goes around, comes around',
are words I feel are very sound,
they convey a need to be more kind,
knowing that you might well find
that you will 'reap what's sown'.

The flipside though is also true,
if there's something you fail to do,
or even if you cause some pain,
there is no reason to complain,
when you 'reap what's sown'.

But there are times we have to learn,
that what went round does not return,
and good or bad turns up for some,
that outweighs anything they've done,
and that's what we call 'Life'.

The Chain of Life

Life's a chain of circumstance,
a challenge to unravel.
Each tip-toed step can spawn regret
as on life's path you travel.

But even if things do look bleak
and you are scared of failing,
the tide can turn, your luck return,
and you end up prevailing.

A trip out of your comfort zone
can make your blood run cold,
but meeting others helps refresh,
restore the you of old.

Sometimes the smallest apertures
allow the sunlight in
and tunes played many moons ago
can spur the heart to sing.

Life's a chain of choices,
linking charms along the way,
decisions made enhance the braid,
plot where we are today.

Overload

I wore the ocean on my shoulders,
a mighty mantle hammering down.
It bore me into rocks and boulders
so many times, I feared I'd drown.

Then I decided not to cower,
to ride the waves and not be ridden,
to saddle them and use their power
and rise above, no longer hidden.

Succour

Cradle the shadows
       grave they may be.

Usher them over
       for sympathy.

Wine them and dine them,
             share secrets and smiles.

Gad in your glad rags
             spend nights on the tiles.

Then in the dawning
             allow them to leave

lifted by lark song
             softly to grieve.

Wild Swimming in a Scottish Pool

No time to dither, just slip in
and feel the rush of cold to heart.
The tingle ripple on the skin
as tadpoles dash and skaters' dart.

Imagine snakes and pirate bones,
'neath murky water mottled green.
Tread water or else toe the stones,
keep mouth clenched tight and drink the scene.

A swooping swallow bids hello
whilst midges gather busily,
the newts are partying below,
like butterflies you're floating free.

Once out, invigoration burns
to jump back in the body yearns.

A Merry Mantra

Turn the page of each new day
Crisp and fresh with life's potential
Sweep those worries clean away
Only carry what's essential

Crisp and fresh with life's potential
Unfurl the curling buds of May
Only carry what's essential
See the sun shine through the grey

Unfurl the curling buds of May
Welcome signs of season's shift
See the sun shine through the grey
Feel the force of freedom lift

Welcome signs of season's shift
Note the courage of green shoots
Feel the force of freedom lift
Gather goodness from wise roots

Note the courage of green shoots
Turn the page of each new day
Gather goodness from wise roots
Sweep those worries clean away

Grow Wild

Grow wild, sweet child
and dip your dainty toes
in groves like troves
swathed in a vibrant green.

Swim strong, stroke long
through waves that tower high,
then fly, through sky
to stars that know your name.

Untame, unframe,
let your heart be beguiled.
Go wild, sweet child
release, relax, restart.

Love Life

I live you yet I wonder where
you get the energy to care.
I breathe your air
and eat your fare
I'm thankful that you freely share.

I live you and I wonder who
inspires everything you do.
So fresh and new
you're never blue
I thank the stars each day for you

I live you and yet I don't know
what waits beyond the next rainbow.
No tell, just show
as on we go
I live you and I love you though.

Summer Dreams

Let loose the dreams of summer
as they emerge you'll see
they strengthen in the sunlight
and multiply when free.

Dreams blossom when you share them
they thrive in company,
let loose the dreams of summer
and watch them come to be.

Dip Trick

Dip a toe into the dunes
June's the month for longer sun
Summer nights host dreamy moons
Moonbeams bathing everyone

One fine day blends with the rest
Rest and relaxation's key
Keys unlock the worry chest
Chest expands as frets fly free

Free to flow and disappear
Peer above the cloud's plump lip
Lip and lap in pools mint clear
Clear out qualms and take a dip

Solar Power

Snap a scene of beauty,
catch it in the sun,
frame it with contentment
share it with someone.

With autumn approaching
let us fill our stores,
ready for the dark days
when we're stuck indoors.

Then we can remember
all the warmth we knew
snap a scene of beauty
it will see you through.

September Sun

This fine September morning
I am sitting in the sun,
inhaling honeysuckle
where spiders spells have spun.

I close my eyes in reverence,
feel goodness on my skin,
brightness smooths my countenance
dispelling doubts within.

This gift to me of mindfulness,
as I bathe in the calm,
filters out irrelevance,
renews me with its charm.

Giving for Life

From deep within the purse is torn,
a new love hatches, sees the dawn,
self-subjugation, nature's norm,
when a child is born.

Joyful, unrelenting, flowing,
telling, showing, ploughing, mowing,
ever harvesting and sowing,
when a child is growing.

Suddenly the nest is flown,
freedom granted, kisses blown,
heart will always be on loan,
when a child is grown.

Harvest of Hope

Gathering, togethering,
assembling and tethering.
Aspects of life that can't help bring
a smile, a glow to faces.

For in these meeting places,
where we are touching bases,
we're fortifying laces
of our humanity.

Community through unity,
affinity glues you and me,
divisions lack their gravity,
when sitting side by side.

As it's impossible to hide,
we must then share, confess, confide
our strengths, our weaknesses and pride
transparently laid bare.

And this is true of everywhere,
as long as we show up, are there,
stay present whether foul or fair
our hearts sing when we're gathering.

The Company of Thought

I never feel alone when I am thinking,
the waves just ebb and flow inside my head.
They sometimes shock, unblock or jog some inking
as I cling on, exploring every thread.

Bleak themes attract me back to gawp, like crime scenes.
'What ifs?' are often pondered, plots are changed.
I analyse what each twist of the knot means –
but it's no more than deckchairs rearranged.

And finding fault of course is where I linger,
my fingers tracing contours, pressing sores.
Exhausted, all my choices face the wringer,
I struggle to keep tally of my flaws.

Walls of my mind replastered and repainted
help me and calm become better acquainted.

Buried Treasure

Memories leak from your cotton wool mind.
Curdle cream flotsam sinks quick into sand.
Facts at your fingertips you used to find,
now out of reach, cordoned off, contraband.

Faces approach with familiar tone
relish referring to recent events
claim they're related to youngsters you've known
– why all the questions that do not make sense?

Let's take a wander down well-trodden paths,
tour of the highlights of life lived so well,
titbits of sadness merge with love and laughs
conjured by images, music and smell.

You're not the you that you used to be
that's why I treasure rare glimpses I see.

A Stoic's View

A stoic's view, though nothing new,
could hold the key to all you do.
As ancient as philosophy,
it challenges and sets you free,
a way to see each crisis through.

So, to your inner self be true,
and follow nature's steadfast cue,
stay positive and aim to see
a stoic's view.

If in your garden no fear grew,
but strength, control and patience too
plus, wisdom in adversity –
knowing that what will be will be
and your response is up to you –
a stoic's view.

The Beginning ... of the End

She was conscious of its lifting
an absence of its weight
quick sands so slowly shifting
tides yearning to abate.

The clouds above were parting
sun striving to peer through
her brain's reboot was starting
and the blindfold slipped off too.

It had been a long time coming
a tunnel damp and dark
the loneliness mind-numbing
ahead seemed grim and stark.

At times, she had despaired
that she would ever smile again
the melancholy flared
and snared her in a vault of pain.

But here at last there was a glow
the beginning of the end
time for her to up and go
with hope her newfound friend.

Daylight Delight

Breathe in the dawn.
The crusty silhouette of night disperses
as dew descends
on sleepy blades,
beads freshly minted petals.

Once inky sky shakes off
the moth munched shroud
through which the universe
blinked twinkly eyed
now out of sight, still watching.

Majestic rise of golden orb
sets rays of sun
to scamper stealthily across the fields.
Teasing the ears of wheat and corn,
orchestrating choruses of song.

We, who trade sleep to meet and greet this new day,
sigh with its signature engraved upon our hearts.

Waxing Lyrical

Champagne a summer cyclone sceptred isle
Dream shards of slithered serpents in the sun
Scale cotton clouds and snuggle in their pile
Bounce in a rainbow castle, just for fun

Charm bracelets jostling to spill their souls
Ride rockets through the universe to peace
Stretch into child's pose o'er burning coals
Hide 'til the Sevillana's strut swirls cease

Meringue a melody with lemon zest
Knit, crochet and cross stitch to pass the time
Dew drop a syllable, refresh your nest
Sing sonnets serenading summit's climb

If breathing starts to trouble you, relax
Then dip your finger into molten wax

Rose Above

Precious me
with rosy
thoughts.
Bloom in my head,
silk dreams.
Float feather clouds,
their downy shrouds
svelte in
the moon's soft beams.

I want a head
that's crystal clear,
with sharp
intensity.
Where beauty
reigns,
in sweet refrains,
and I'm
where I should be.

Dismantle thorns,
and thoughts
that prick.
Let all conflicts
subside.
As worries cease
I just want peace
on sunset kissed
moon tide.

Wise Flowers

My walk takes a path
where the wildflowers go,
        grow straight to the light
                        and keep going.

Their seeds have been scattered
in soils far and wide,
        they beat all the odds
                        never slowing.

Mixed bunches of beauty,
scents summon the bees,
        who feast as if there's
                        no tomorrow.

My walk takes a path
where the wise flowers show,
        a hardy example
                        to follow.

If Only...

If only I had known
If only I had seen
If only I had listened
If only I had been
If only I had felt
If only I had thought
If only I had tried
If only I had sought

'If only I had' doesn't change
the me I am today
although sometimes reflection
helps explain life's twisty way.

In years to come, when I look back
on all that's gone before,
if I have only done my best
I cannot ask for more.

Sonnet to do

I take a stroll in shade and shelter,
from the weather's wild affray.
The gutsy dog with rusty pelt, a
panting partner, plots the way.

Through tangled yews strewn yesteryear
our steps peruse the path.
Distilling clues, ferns gesture near,
a cleansing nature bath.

So, to the meadow's pulsing lifeline,
shiver grass and bumble,
we saunter home re-tuned, in chime,
from bigger picture, humble.

The daily walk, sometimes a chore,
reveals fresh pastures to explore.

I Dwell in Possibility

(after Emily Dickinson)

I dwell in Possibility
Each Dawn, a fresh Surprise
My Future Path unwritten
Beneath uncharted Skies

My House has many Windows
Each Room an unlocked Door
No Roof except the Heavens
Carte Blanche to just explore

A welcome Stream of Visitors
Step up and roll the Dice
First blow and make a single Wish
To live in Paradise

Divine Midnight

This sacred hour slices through night,
your yesterday's soon out of sight.

A velvet curtain on the scene,
dense black and comforting, serene.

From now all clocks will be reset,
tomorrow can be your best yet.

So, take the time to simply breathe,
let peace invade and turmoil leave.

This hour's divine and holds the key,
divides what's been from what will be.

Tea for Two

Pour me a cup of Forget-Me-Not tea
　　　　it's time to remember the past.

Trace all the fingers who've gripped here before,
　　　　smile knowing mine won't be last.

Breathe in the peace of the steam that's released,
　　　　sip at the lips long departed.

Imbibe the vibe of serenity brought
　　　　by being kind and warm hearted.

Toast the good health of all we hold dear.
　　　　Thank all the stars in the sky.

Pour me a cup of Forget-Me-Not tea
　　　　for this is 'hello' not 'goodbye'.

Serene Moon Scene

I've never seen the sea so still
and still the scene I saw
was more serene than any
that's been set 'fore me before.

The full moon burst with clarity
and clearly it soon spilled
spooned deep into the shiny sheen
I swooned, as my pulse stilled.

Early Praise
for *Rhymes For The Mind*

A lovely, worthwhile and comforting collection. It shows a wonderful range and gives the reader plenty to choose from, with solace and encouragement for all kinds of mental and emotional experiences. It's poetry with purpose, offering a guiding hand back to joy and contentment. *Liz Kendall*

In this uplifting latest collection, Sharron Green's poems brim over with natural warmth. Light, sunshine and the hope of spring burst through these heartfelt verses. Upbeat and positive, they remind us that the glass half-empty is also always half-full, and that life can be a magical gift, if only we choose to recognize it. Here too is a poet who revels in rhyme and structure giving us a dazzling tour of poetic forms ranging from circular pieces that joyfully 'loop the loop' to skilful sonnets. Sharron celebrates the ordinary routines and everyday spaces we all inhabit and encourages us, with much charm and wit, to look at the world with fresh eyes and embrace the wonder of it all. *Jeremy Loynes*

Beautifully woven—Sharron Green is a wordsmith of rhymes. Have a cup of tea with her and her poetry book. Sit down and drink her 'Forget-Me-Not tea' and fall in love with her rhymes as I did. Her words are poignant, her poems ease the mind. Life is about all the emotions—about the sad and beautiful alike. She plays with forms and words and invites us to 'dip a toe into the dunes'. We dive with her into the ocean 'no need to choose a port'. I feel free while reading. Sharron speaks to my heart. And moves me gently. *Miriam Otto*

Acknowledgements

I'm fortunate to say that with each year my debt of gratitude for support and inspiration grows. Having started at home, with husband Kevin and son Sam, it now extends to friends, family and poetry groups throughout the U.K. and overseas.

My fellow Booming Lovelies—Heather Moulson and Trisha Broomfield—offer daily feedback and encouragement. In addition, Sarah Drury, Victoria D'Cruz, Alice Fowler and Liz Kendall are also always on hand with advice and help with poetry events and opportunities.

Thanks to Liz Kendall, Jeremy Loynes and Miriam Otto, my early readers, whose enthusiasm for Rhymes for the Mind has been hugely reassuring on this journey to publication.

Eternal thanks to Reena Doss of Ink Gladiators Press for helping with formatting, cover design and publishing and amazing support with my other titles.

As always, I'd like to show appreciation to the Instagram poetry community for their inventiveness & inspiration. Particularly the following accounts, some of which prompted the poems shared here:

@altpoetryprompts
@ajbutlerwriting
@coralynn.poetry
@darakalima
@gwensaintmary
@inksomnia_poetry
@lindalokheeauthor
@lrsterlingpoetry
@mikejdennis5

@ml_macdonald_
@neha.m.taneja
@officialsurreynwfest
@poeticreveries_
@poetrybattles
@randomerbobsxyz
@themumpoempress
@truculentbutamiable
@yaffle.press

About the Author

Sharron Green's work blends nostalgia, nature and comments on modern life, gaining her a strong and loyal following on social media—where she's better known as Rhymes_n_Roses.

In addition to her three other chapbooks – *Introducing Rhymes_n_Roses*, *Viral Odes* and *Willing Words* – Sharron has individual poems in over 20 international anthologies.

A confident and skilled performance poet, Sharron co-hosts two open mic poetry nights – Poetry & Pizza at Solar Sisters in Guildford and Write Out Loud at the Fiery Bird Venue Woking. She is also a proud member of the Booming Lovelies, a trio of poets who have performed at venues around Surrey and in London.

In 2022, she graduated with an MA in Creative Writing from the University of Surrey and was a Head Writer for the Surrey New Writers Festival in 2023.

Sharron lives with her husband and golden retriever Dougie in Guildford and enjoys walking in the beautiful Surrey Hills – a landscape that often inspires her poetry.

Instagram, Facebook, Threads, X & TikTok: @rhymes_n_roses
Website: https://rhymesnroses.com

Hattie Stewart-Darling © Photography

Printed in Great Britain
by Amazon

58544861R00030